Words by Norman C. Habel
Pictures by Jim Roberts

The King Who Was A Clown

A PURPLE PUZZLE TREE BOOK
COPYRIGHT © 1972 CONCORDIA PUBLISHING HOUSE, ST. LOUIS, MISSOURI
CONCORDIA PUBLISHING HOUSE LTD., LONDON, E. C. 1
MANUFACTURED IN THE UNITED STATES OF AMERICA
ISBN 0-570-06518-6

Concordia Publishing House

On Easter day, if you were king,
Would you let God's people swing?
Would you let them laugh and sing
If you were king?

If you were king do you believe
That you would have a New Year's Eve
With choc'late whistles up your sleeve,
If you were the king?

And would you have a circus grand
Twice as big as Disneyland
With acrobats and a one clown band,
If you were king?

When David became king, he said:
"I need a palace and throne,
a big and beautiful city
where I can be God's clown
and celebrate His name."

So the people said, "Jerusalem!
Now that's a jazzy place,
a tall, white, gleaming town,
just like a queen from heaven
in a glittering silver gown.

"And the middle of Jerusalem
is the middle of the world,
where the middle of the heaven
meets the middle of the earth."

The people who lived in old Jerusalem
were jumpy Jebusites.

The Jebusites kept crying, "Boo!
Boo, David, Boo!
Your tricks will never do.
Our walls are all so strong and thick
a blind man sitting on the wall
could kill you with his little stick
as you try to burrow through."

Now David was a rascal
long before he was a king,
and he had learned a trick or two
while having his little fling.

David knew about a tunnel
that went underneath the wall.
It was an underground passage,
dark and deep and dirty,
that led into a little well
in the center of the city.

David and his men
crawled slowly through the tunnel,
SPLISH SPLOSH,
SPLISH SPLOSH, YUK!
Soon their bodies were covered
with white and orange muck,
SPLISH SPLOSH,
SPLISH SPLOSH, YUK!

They looked like men from Mars,
or maybe men from hell,
as they rushed out through that hole
in the middle of the town.
They jumped the jumpy Jebusites,
who ran like scared cats
when they saw the mighty, muddy David
and his funny, muddy ghosts.

David loved Jersualem
and made it a fortress town
that would never, never fall
and never, never fall down.

When the New Year came,
David planned to celebrate
and tell the world
his God was really great.
He went out to a country town
where the old, old ark was kept.
The ark was like a golden throne
high above a box,
where men would come
to feel God give them power
before they went back home.

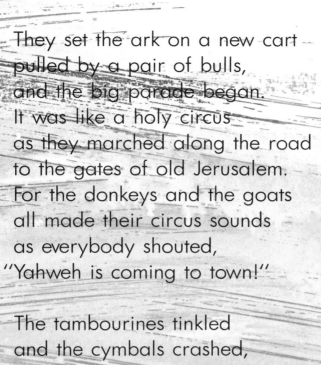

They set the ark on a new cart
pulled by a pair of bulls,
and the big parade began.
It was like a holy circus
as they marched along the road
to the gates of old Jerusalem.
For the donkeys and the goats
all made their circus sounds
as everybody shouted,
"Yahweh is coming to town!"

The tambourines tinkled
and the cymbals crashed,
the harp strings plinkled
and the golden ark flashed
as they danced and sang
all the way to Jerusalem.

There were wild, red kites
that played with God in the sky,
and floating banners that read:
YAHWEH IS KING ON HIGH!

David the king
was the biggest clown of all,
for he was really the priest
who led the people in worship
till everyone was blessed.

David leaped and danced
as if he were a bird.
He flung his royal robes
like gifts up to the Lord,
until he stood there praising God,
a free and naked clown.

Then suddenly
one of the bulls that pulled the ark
stumbled and almost fell.
And one of the men who drove the cart
grabbed the side of the ark.

And just like that,
quick as a cat,
there came an "electric" shock.
The man was dead...
dead as a rock.

So the people understood
that the ark is very holy,
and you can never handle it
like any other box.
And some of them remembered
a song they used to sing:

Our God is not a Jack-in-the-box
Who pops and stops and stops and pops.
You cannot wind Him like a clock
Until He stops and pops and stops.

When they reached Jerusalem
David pitched a tent for the ark.
He set it on the mount of God,
which is the middle of the world,
where the middle of the heaven
meets the middle of the earth.
And there,
precisely there,
God blessed the whole, wide world
and made it new again that day
like a big, bright, shiny ball.

As the people gathered around the ark,
they ate the bread of God
and sang a song like this:

Our God is not Aladdin's lamp
That gives you ev'ry wish you wish.
You cannot swish Him with a cloth
To swish a wish and wish a swish!

Our God is not a tiddelee toy,
But sends His love in rain and sun.
So dance around the center of earth
As God remakes the world for fun.

Do you like to worship God that way
and watch Him making the world
with His sun and moon and rays
in the middle of the earth,
especially on New Year's Day?

David loved his God so much
he wanted to build Him a temple.
But God had other plans:
"David, I love you, I do.
And I promise you now and forever
your sons will rule on your throne.
One of your sons will build Me a temple,
a house that men will call Mine.
But if your sons don't follow Me,
I'll have to bring them in line."

That was the promise to David
and part of the purple puzzle,
a plan to bless all men
and bring them back to God.

One of the sons of David the Clown,
over a thousand years later,
was born in the town
where David was born
and became the King of all men.

And I'm sure He still rules
on the throne of God today—
in the middle of the world,
which isn't far away!

Aren't you?

OTHER TITLES

the PURPLE PUZZLE TREE